MESSAGES
ON THE
MOON

BY **JILL FRIESTAD-TATE**

ILLUSTRATED BY
MICHAEL PAUSTIAN

www.BookpressPublishing.com

In July of 1969, people all over the world watched with anticipation. No one had ever walked on the Moon. In fact, no one in history had successfully landed on the Moon. The astronauts of the Apollo 11 mission hoped to do both.

Before takeoff, NASA planned a celebration. NASA wanted the astronauts to leave several items on the Moon.

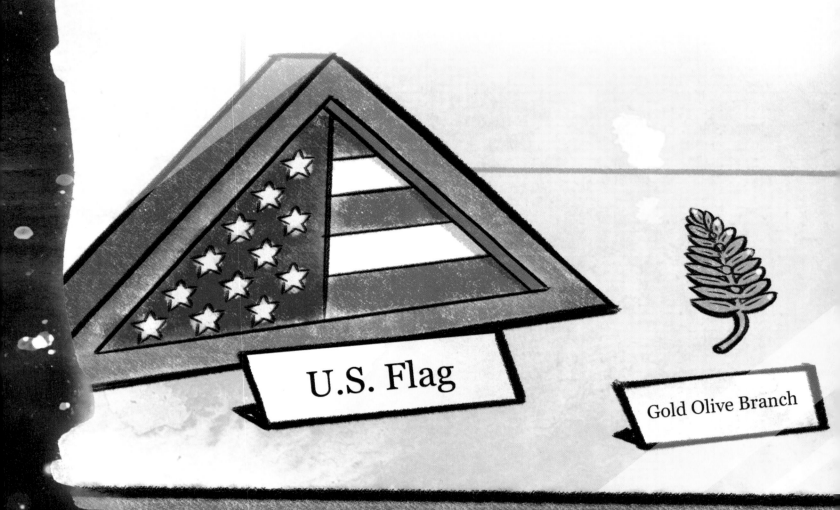

U.S. Flag

Gold Olive Branch

One month before the launch, NASA had another idea. They asked 116 world leaders to send messages of peace that would be left on the Moon. Also included were messages from four United States presidents, names of the members of Congress, and NASA employees. The messages would show others that the mission was peaceful. NASA received messages from many countries.

But NASA had a problem. They didn't know how to protect the messages from being damaged on the Moon. Sprague Electric Company was asked to find a way to protect them.

Paper was not strong enough.

Microfilm would fall apart.

And then they found it—a silicon disc!

The silicon disc was the size of a half dollar coin.
The messages were reduced to the size of a pin head.

Sprague Electric Company fit the countries' goodwill wishes onto the disc. Two weeks before lift-off, more messages were sent to NASA, and the disc had to be remade. The final disc was finished just five days before being flown to the Moon!

On July 16, 1969, the Apollo 11 astronauts lifted off from Cape Kennedy as the world watched. The flight was a success. After a few days in space, the astronauts were ready to land on the Moon.

Neil Armstrong flew the lunar module, Eagle. Alarms beeped as he and Buzz Aldrin tried to land. The control room in Houston, Texas, started to worry. But Armstrong remained calm.

After a few minutes, Armstrong reported back to Mission Control, "Houston, Tranquility Base here. The Eagle has landed." All over the world, people breathed a sigh of relief.

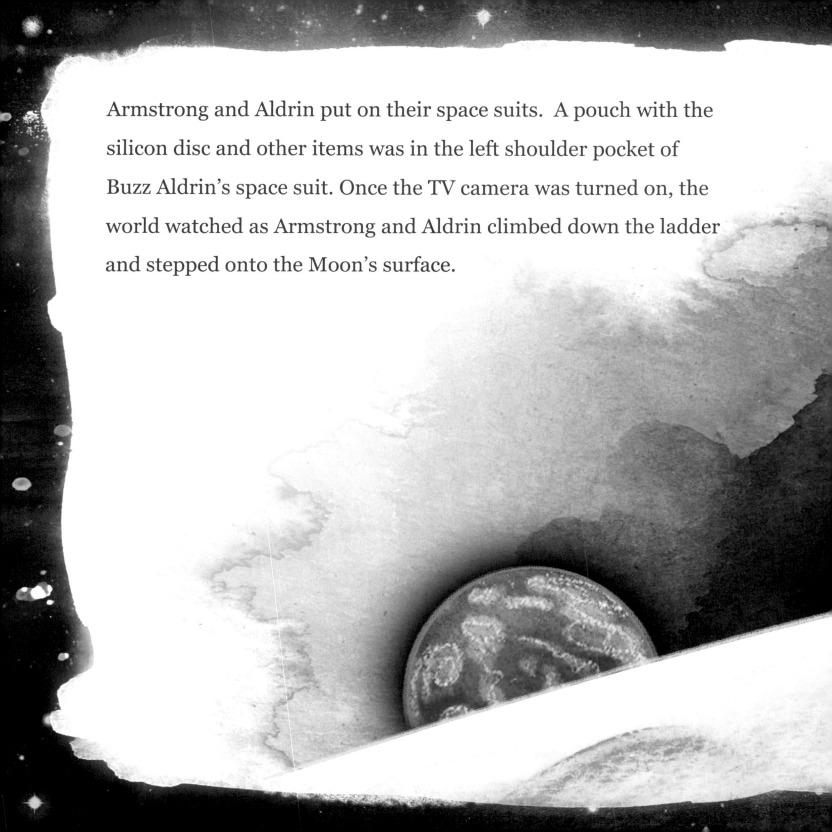

Armstrong and Aldrin put on their space suits. A pouch with the silicon disc and other items was in the left shoulder pocket of Buzz Aldrin's space suit. Once the TV camera was turned on, the world watched as Armstrong and Aldrin climbed down the ladder and stepped onto the Moon's surface.

That's one small step for a man, one giant leap for mankind.
UNITED STATES

Celebrations erupted around the world! In Poland, an 11-year old boy stayed up late to watch TV.

In Northern Ireland, a shepherd listened to the news on a radio as he tended his sheep.

In Cairo, a man selling leather goods ran through the streets sharing the good news.

At sea, an Italian captain and his crew gathered around a transistor radio to hear the news.

In France, people celebrated with expensive champagne.

In England, a school teacher smiled as he sipped his tea.

In Romania, a furniture maker skipped work to visit the local library and read space books.

People with radios and televisions were able to witness the Moon landing, but some did not know it happened. Over 750 million people in China were not told.

Russian radio tried to block stations so people could not hear the news. But people found unjammed radio stations and listened anyway. Hearing that U.S. astronauts left medals of Russian cosmonauts, Komaro and Gagarin, on the Moon made them feel proud.

Back on the Moon, Armstrong and Aldrin had work to do.
One of their first jobs was to place the U.S. flag on the Moon.
They also read the plaque on the lunar module to TV viewers,
received a phone call from the President of the United States,
conducted scientific experiments, and collected 48 pounds
of lunar dust and rocks.

Armstrong and Aldrin finished their work and started to board the Eagle. They almost forgot to leave the pouch with goodwill messages on the Moon! As Aldrin climbed the ladder to board the Eagle, Armstrong reminded him.

Aldrin tossed the pouch with the silicon disc and other items on the Moon's surface. Armstrong moved it to clear off the Moon dust. He paused to recognize the disc's message of peace and hope during a time when the world celebrated together.

...the disc with the messages was placed on the surface as planned.

An American flag, the lunar module base, scientific instruments, and the silicon disc stayed on the Moon. Armstrong and Aldrin climbed aboard the Eagle and lifted off the Moon's surface. With their mission complete, the Apollo 11 astronauts headed back to Earth.

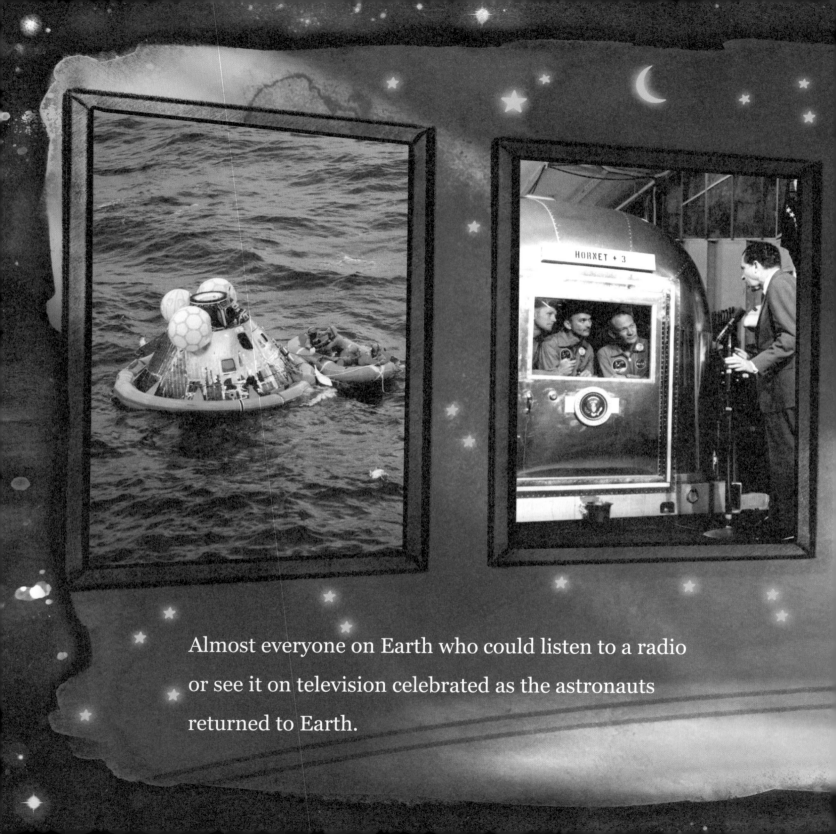

Almost everyone on Earth who could listen to a radio
or see it on television celebrated as the astronauts
returned to Earth.

A small silicon disc symbolizes the only time in history that the world joined together in celebration. Someday, others will land on the Moon and find a silicon disc in the lunar soil that reads, "From Plant Earth (1969)". Using a microscope, they will read good wishes from world leaders. What will be the next event to unite the world in hope and peace?

GOODWILL MESSAGES FROM AROUND THE WORLD

United States

"...Here is testimony to man's vision and to man's courage. The journey of the astronauts is more than a technical achievement; it is a reaching-out of the human spirit. It lifts our sights...They inspire us and at the same time they teach us true humility. What could bring home to us more the limitations of the human scale than the hauntingly beautiful picture of our Earth seen from the Moon?"

— President Richard M. Nixon

Australia

"...May the high courage and the technical genius which made this achievement possible be so used in the future that mankind will live in a universe in which peace, self-expression, and the chance of dangerous adventure are available to all."

— John Gorton, Prime Minister

Brazil

"...In rejoicing together with the government and the people of the United States of America for the event of the century, I pray God that this brilliant achievement of science remain always at the service of peace and of mankind."

— Arthur Da Costa E Silva, President

Canada

"Man has reached out and touched the tranquil Moon. May that high accomplishment allow man to rediscover the Earth and find peace."

– Pierre Elliott-Trudeau, Prime Minister

Japan

"In congratulation of the outstanding achievement of humanity's arrival on the Moon.."

– Eisaku Sato, Prime Minister

Ghana

"We pray that your historic landing on the Moon may usher in an era of peace and prosperity and goodwill among all men here on Earth."

– Brigadier A. A. Afrifa, D.S.O., Chairman, National Liberation Council

United Kingdom

"On behalf of the British people I salute the skill and courage which have brought man to the Moon. May this endeavor increase the knowledge and well-being of mankind."

– Elizabeth R. (Queen Elizabeth II)

Associated Press (1969, July 22). Earth beaming over mastery of moon. Omaha World Herald, pp. 5.

Hanion, M. (2019). Apollo 11 brought a message of peace to the Moon—but Neil and Buzz almost forgot to leave it behind. Retrieved on 11 July 2019 from: https://phys.org/news/2019-03-apollo-brought-message-peace-moonbut.html.

NASA Mission Report (n.d.). Retrieved on 11 July 2019 from: https://www.hq.nasa.gov/alsj/a11/A11_PAOMissionReport.html.

NASA (1969). Apollo 11 goodwill messages. Retrieved on 11 July 2019 from: https://history.nasa.gov/ap11-35ann/goodwill/Apollo_11_material.pdf.

Pearlman, R. (2007). The untold story: How one small disc carried one giant message for mankind. Retrieved 11 July 2019 from: https://www.space.com/4655-untold-story-small-disc-carried-giant-message-mankind.html.

Rahman, T. (2008). We came in peace for all mankind: The untold story of the Apollo 11 silicon disc. Leathers Publishing: Overland Park, Kansas.

Published in Des Moines, Iowa, by:
Bookpress Publishing • P.O. Box 71532, Des Moines, IA 50325
www.BookpressPublishing.com

Publisher's Cataloging-in-Publication Data

Names: Friestad-Tate, Jill, author.
Title: Messages on the Moon / Jill Friestad-Tate.
Description: Des Moines, IA: BookPress Publishing, 2021.
Identifiers: LCCN: 2021900149 | ISBN: 978-1-947305-30-4
Subjects: LCSH Project Apollo (U.S.)--Juvenile literature. | Space flight to the moon--History--Juvenile literature. | Space race--United States--Juvenile literature. | CYAC Project Apollo (U.S.) | Space flight to the moon. | Space race. | JUVENILE NONFICTION / History / United States / 20th Century | JUVENILE NONFICTION / Technology / Aeronautics, Astronautics & Space Science
Classification: LCC TL789.8.U6 A5813 2021 | DDC 629.45/4/0973--dc23

First Edition

Printed in the United States of America
10 9 8 7 6 5 4 3 2 1